I CAN
READ ABOUT

SEASONS

Written by Robyn Supraner

Illustrated by Gloria McKeown

Troll Associates

10 9 8 7 6 5 4 3 2

This is a
story of the
seasons. It is a
story of mystery and
adventure. It is a story of
change. For the earth is on a journey
that never ends—
a spinning, whirling trip around the blazing sun.

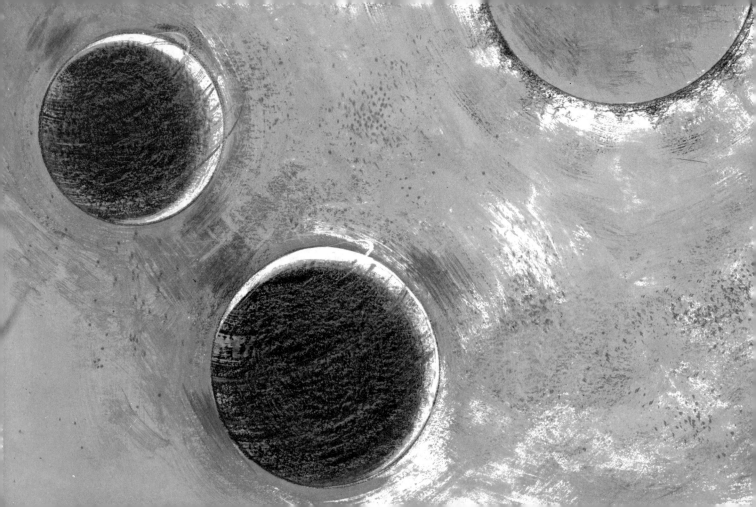

Like a giant top,
the earth speeds through space.
Sometimes, it tips towards the sun.
Sometimes, it tips away.
And as it spins, the seasons come.
And as it tips, the seasons go.
Summer. Autumn. Winter. Spring.

Day and night, month after month,
the earth follows the same oval path.
It takes about 365 days to complete a
single trip around the sun. And when that
is done, a new trip begins. Spinning and whirling,
the earth continues on its way. Around and around.
Summer. Autumn. Winter . . .

Spring.
A time of beginning.
A time of new life. As the
earth tips towards the sun, the
days begin to grow longer. Sunshine
melts the last snow and thaws the
frozen ground.

Crocuses pop up.
Sap rises in the trees.
Once again, thirsty roots
carry food and water
to branches
and buds.

April showers fall gently.
Worms make tunnels through the
earth. Buds grow fat and burst
into flower. Leaves cover the trees.

It is time for the birds, who travelled south for the winter, to return to their summer homes in the North. It is time for migration.

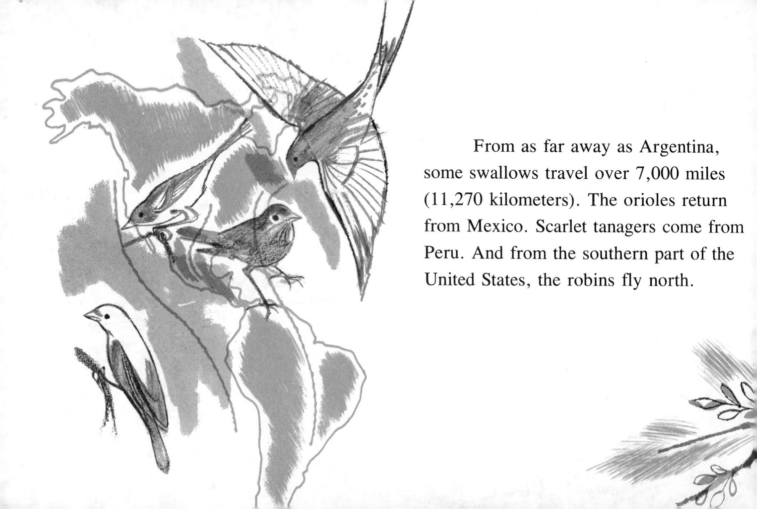

From as far away as Argentina, some swallows travel over 7,000 miles (11,270 kilometers). The orioles return from Mexico. Scarlet tanagers come from Peru. And from the southern part of the United States, the robins fly north.

The birds have returned to their
warm-weather homes to build their
nests, lay their eggs, and
raise their babies.

The worms and insects and berries, that will be needed to feed them, are already growing and hatching and multiplying.

When the time comes, there will be plenty for all.

Farmers turn
the soil and plant
seeds in the fresh earth.
Spring is a time for sowing.

It is a time
of birth.

Tiny rabbits blink their eyes and
breathe the sweet spring air. They are
getting their first look at the world.

Young lambs leap and play in the green meadow.

A cow licks her new calf.
Baby piglets lie near their mother.
Their stomachs are full and they are
squealing happily. The ducklings turn
around and answer with a quacking sound.

They all seem to be saying,
"Spring is here! Spring is here!"

Around and around
spins the earth.

Now the North Pole is as close
to the sun as it will get. Today is
the longest day of the year. In the
northern half of the world, summer has begun.

The days are long and hot and lazy. In time, the farmer's seeds begin to bear fruit. Cucumbers and carrots and tomatoes are ready to be picked.

Flower gardens burst with bloom.
Daisies and roses hold up their heads
to the golden sunshine.

The ducklings lose their soft, fuzzy
fluff. Each day they look more like their
mothers and fathers.

The animals are getting bigger and stronger.
They romp in the meadow and bask in
the sun. While they are playing,
they are learning. Summer is
a time of ripening.

Butterflies flit and flutter.
You can see orange monarchs, and small
white cabbage butterflies, and black
swallowtails dancing in the
summer air.

Honeybees swarm and gather pollen.
Honey must be made and the young must be
fed. New fields must be found. The
bees are very busy.
Summer is the season
of their lives.

Most schools are closed. Children are on vacation. It is time to swim and hike. It is time to go camping. Time to dream. Time to explore.

Around and around spins the earth. One day the leaves are turning orange and yellow and flaming red. The North Pole tips farther and farther away from the sun. Gradually, the days grow shorter. The long, dreamy days of summer are over. Autumn is here!

There is a chill in the air. Flocks of robins settle on the branches of trees. Swallows gather on telephone wires. Everywhere, hungry birds cheep and chatter. It is time for the fall migration. Time for the birds to go south, where the weather is warm.

Clouds of orange and black butterflies join the migration.
Some of them will fly all the way from Canada
to Mexico.

Chipmunks and squirrels
dart here and there. Their
cheeks are bulging with nuts and
seeds. They are busy burying acorns.
Winter is coming!

A caterpillar
clings to a branch. It is spinning
a cocoon. It will spend the long, cold months
ahead wrapped in silken threads.
Autumn is a time of getting ready.

Grapes hang heavy on
the vine. The trees
are thick with golden
pears and rosy apples.

Pumpkins, fat and orange,
lie ripening in the sun.

Fields of corn are ready for the harvest. Autumn is a time of reaping.

Around and around spins the earth. It has been autumn for a long time. The trees are bare. The weeds and flowers are withered.

The North Pole has tipped far away
from the sun. Today is the shortest
day of the year. Autumn is over.
Winter is here.

Snow falls.

It fills the empty birds' nests.

It covers the trees and houses with a white blanket.

When the sun shines, some of the snow melts.

Later, when it is colder, the melting
snow freezes into glassy icicles.

Not all the birds have gone south.
Blue jays, cardinals and sparrows call
to each other. They gather at the
feeders and argue over crumbs. Their
feet leave little tracks
in the snow.

The frogs have gone to the bottom
of the pond to stay warm.

Woodchucks and bears go to sleep.
They will spend the short days and the long nights
curled up in their cozy dens.

The frost has killed
most of the insects, but their eggs
are safe beneath the snow. Some eggs hang
in papery cocoons. Others stay dry
in a hollow log.

When spring returns,
the eggs will hatch. A new life cycle
will begin. Winter is a time of
waiting.

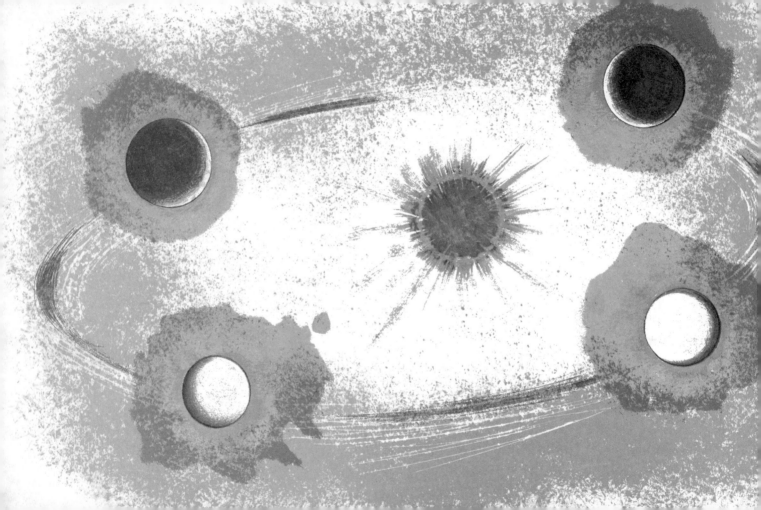

Around and around spins the earth.
The seasons come. The seasons go. Winter.
Spring. Summer. Autumn.
Around and around. The mysterious and
wonderful trip never ends.